HONDURAS

...in Pictures

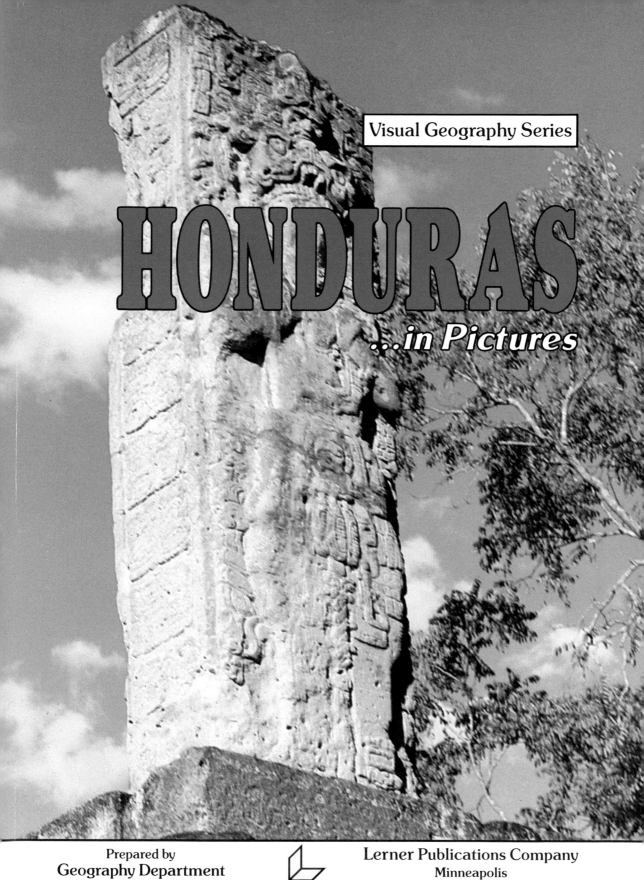

Visual Geography Series

HONDURAS

...in Pictures

Prepared by
Geography Department

Lerner Publications Company
Minneapolis

Independent Picture Service

In rural areas, Hondurans often live in one-room thatched huts.

This is an all-new edition of the Visual Geography Series. Previous editions have been published by Sterling Publishing Company, New York City, and some of the original textual information has been retained. New photographs, maps, charts, captions, and updated information have been added. The text has been entirely reset in 10/12 Century Textbook.

LIBRARY OF CONGRESS CATALOGING-IN-PUBLICATION DATA

Honduras in pictures.

(Visual geography series)
Rev. ed. of: Honduras in pictures / prepared by Ken Weddle.
Includes index.
Summary: Text and pictures provide a close look at the land, people, history, government, and economy of this Central American nation.
1. Honduras. [1. Honduras] I. Weddle, Ken. Honduras in pictures. II. Lerner Publications Company. Geography Dept. III. Series: Visual geography series (Minneapolis, Minn.)
F1503.H76 1987   972.83   86–15232
ISBN 0-8225-1804-X (lib. bdg.)

International Standard Book Number: 0-8225-1805-8
Library of Congress Catalog Card Number: 86–20029

VISUAL GEOGRAPHY SERIES

Publisher
Harry Jonas Lerner
Associate Publisher
Nancy M. Campbell
Executive Series Editor
Lawrence J. Zwier
Assistant Series Editor
Mary M. Rodgers
Editorial Assistant
Nora W. Kniskern
Illustrations Editor
Nathan A. Haverstock
Consultants/Contributors
Dr. Ruth F. Hale
Nathan A. Haverstock
Sandra K. Davis
Designer
Jim Simondet
Cartographer
Carol F. Barrett
Indexer
Kristine S. Schubert
Production Manager
Richard J. Hannah

Courtesy of David Mangurian

A young girl peeks from behind the door of her house in a Tegucigalpa slum.

Acknowledgments
Title page photo courtesy of Costa Rican Information Service.

Elevation contours adapted from *The Times Atlas of the World,* seventh comprehensive edition (New York: Times Books, 1985).

3 4 5 6 7 8 9 10 96 95 94 93 92 91 90 89 88

Courtesy of Inter-American Development Bank

Grapefruit seedlings are weeded by hand at a project nursery in the Aguán Valley of northern Honduras. The experimental station is part of a government-financed, agrarian-reform program that hopes to cultivate 100,000 acres of cooperative farmland.

Contents

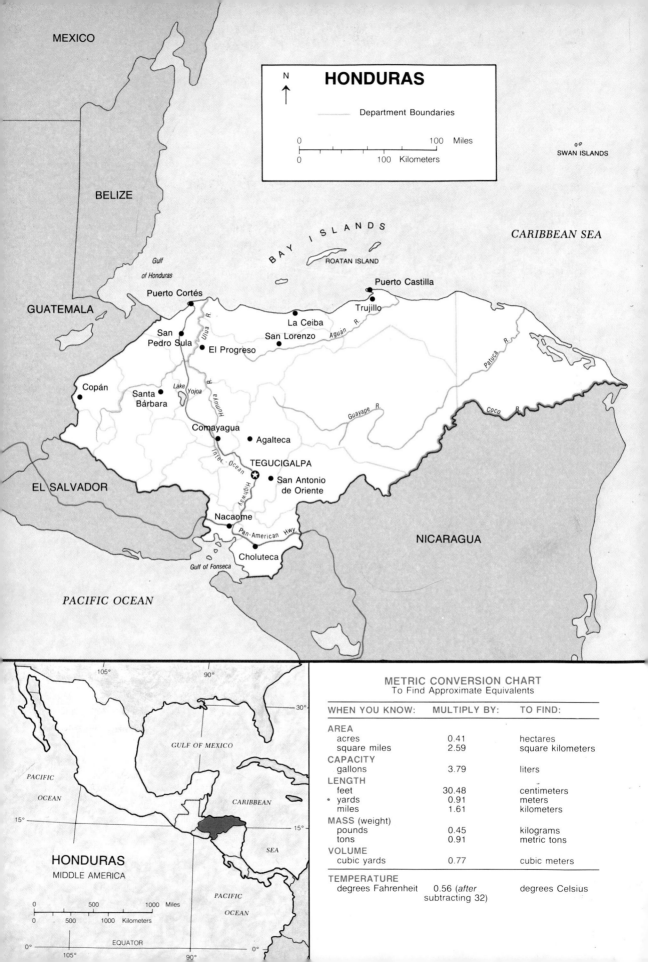

MEXICO

BELIZE

GUATEMALA

N ↑

HONDURAS

—— Department Boundaries

0   100 Miles

0   100 Kilometers

oo
SWAN ISLANDS

B A Y I S L A N D S

CARIBBEAN SEA

ROATAN ISLAND

Gulf of Honduras

Puerto Castilla

Puerto Cortés

Trujillo

Ulua R.

La Ceiba

San
Pedro Sula

San Lorenzo

Aguan R.

El Progreso

Patuca R.

Copán

Santa
Bárbara

Lake
Yojoa

Humuya R.

Guayape R.

Coco R.

Comayagua

Agalteca

Inter.-Ocean

TEGUCIGALPA

San Antonio
de Oriente

Highway

EL SALVADOR

NICARAGUA

Nacaome

Pan-American Hwy

Choluteca

Gulf of Fonseca

PACIFIC OCEAN

105°   90°

30°

GULF OF MEXICO

PACIFIC

OCEAN

CARIBBEAN

15°   15°

SEA

HONDURAS

MIDDLE AMERICA

PACIFIC

OCEAN

0   500   1000 Miles

0   500   1000 Kilometers

EQUATOR   0°

105°   90°

METRIC CONVERSION CHART
To Find Approximate Equivalents

WHEN YOU KNOW:	MULTIPLY BY:	TO FIND:
AREA		
acres	0.41	hectares
square miles	2.59	square kilometers
CAPACITY		
gallons	3.79	liters
LENGTH		
feet	30.48	centimeters
• yards	0.91	meters
miles	1.61	kilometers
MASS (weight)		
pounds	0.45	kilograms
tons	0.91	metric tons
VOLUME		
cubic yards	0.77	cubic meters
TEMPERATURE		
degrees Fahrenheit	0.56 (*after* subtracting 32)	degrees Celsius

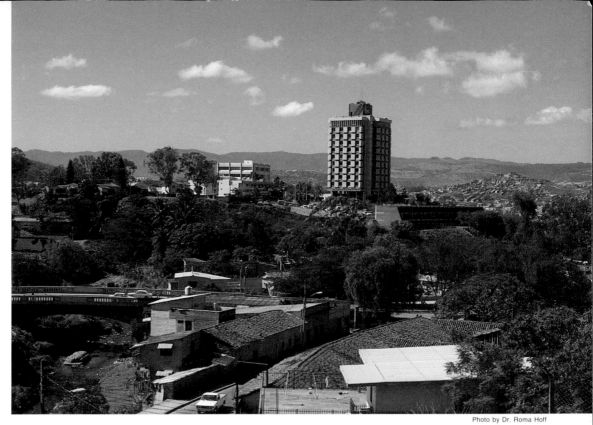

The tallest building in the Honduran capital of Tegucigalpa is the Hotel Maya that overlooks the city's green hills and red-tiled roofs. Much of Tegucigalpa's architecture recalls its Spanish colonial past.

Introduction

At first, a visitor to Honduras may sense only that the statistics are right—that it is one of the poorest nations in the Western Hemisphere. Honduras's average income per person is $560, and its foreign debt amounts to $9.2 million. Almost 50 percent of the nation's population is under the age of 15, and at the current growth rate—3.1 percent—the number of Hondurans will double in 22 years. Over two-thirds of Honduras has no access to safe drinking water, and its infant mortality rate—69 deaths in every 1,000 births—is one of the highest in Central America.

Compared to the restless energy exhibited by their neighbors—the Salvadorans and the Nicaraguans—Hondurans appear to lack drive. Life seems to flow at a leisurely pace—even in the downtown areas of the capital city, Tegucigalpa. Here, businesspeople often make their calls on foot, which contributes to the general sense of quiet that visitors notice.

These impressions are deceptive, however. Hondurans, consciously and with firm determination, are seeking to preserve a sense of the human scale of life. The country has not rushed to build huge hotels or airports to accommodate the largest jets. Nor have the tranquil settings of the nation's villages—surrounded by mountains in fertile valleys—changed very much.

Despite these concerted attempts to lead a quiet life, Hondurans have become involved in the violent events of Central America. By 1984 five armies (including their own) were operating within Honduran territory. The most powerful were the U.S. forces that, as of 1987, were still staging large-scale land and naval maneuvers.

Much less welcome were the Nicaraguan government forces and their opponents, the rebel contras, who have tangled intermittently along the Honduran border. Most irksome of all were the Salvadoran troops who were receiving guerrilla warfare training from U.S. instructors on Honduran soil. (At the request of the Honduran government, the United States stopped using Honduras as a training ground for Salvadoran soldiers.)

The children of Honduras represent its future and its greatest natural resource.

In August 1987 Honduran president José Azcona Hoyo—along with the chief executives of Nicaragua, El Salvador, Costa Rica, and Guatemala—signed a peace initiative in Guatemala City. Dubbed the Guatemala Accord, the plan is designed to defuse the regional conflicts that ravage Central America.

According to the accord, cease-fires will be called in all civil wars in the area, foreign aid to rebel groups will stop, and free elections will be held. Part of the plan also calls for ejecting the contras from their bases in Honduras and sending them back to Nicaragua. With years of turmoil behind it, Honduras hopes that this new plan—supported by the main participants in the tensions that have torn the area— will succeed and will allow Hondurans to resume their pursuit of a quiet lifestyle.

In the capital, just below the fortified walls of the Presidential Palace, women wash clothes in the Choluteca River.

8

The mountainous landscape of Honduras is dotted with dormant volcanoes and covers 80 percent of the country's surface area.

1) The Land

The Republic of Honduras is located near the middle of the long isthmus that connects Mexico with South America. Among the nations of Central America it ranks second in size, with an area of 43,277 square miles. Shaped somewhat like a triangle, it has a maximum north-to-south distance of approximately 200 miles and a maximum east-to-west distance of about 400 miles.

Honduras has a 400-mile-long northern seacoast on the Caribbean Sea, and to the south it fronts about 40 miles of the Gulf of Fonseca—an inlet of the Pacific Ocean. It is bordered on the southwest by El Salvador and on the west by Guatemala. To the south and east, it shares a long border with Nicaragua.

The Highlands

With approximately 80 percent of its surface area composed of volcanic mountains, high plateaus, and rolling hills, Honduras is the most mountainous of the Central American countries. The volcanoes are no longer active, but the difficulty of building adequate roads and communication facilities through them has impeded the nation's economic development. The highest point in the country is in the Montaña de Celaque, one of the many ranges in the southwest, where volcanic peaks reach an elevation of 9,400 feet.

About 70 percent of the nation's population is concentrated in the highlands, which extend from Guatemala to Nicaragua and comprise about 65 percent of the

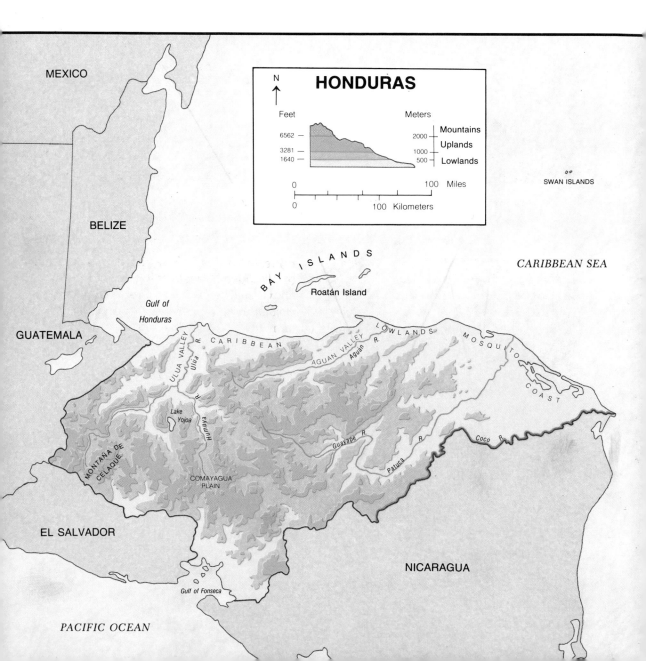

Until recently, many of Honduras's economic difficulties could be traced to its mountainous terrain, which impeded the building of roads for commerce, agriculture, and communications.

The lush green valleys of the highlands produce most of the maize consumed in Honduras.

nation's total land area. This region, lying at altitudes between 2,000 and 5,000 feet above sea level, has a moderate climate throughout the year. Between the ranges of mountains are rolling green valleys with fertile soil derived from volcanic ash and lava deposits. This region produces practically all of the nation's coffee, potatoes, wheat, maize, fruits, beans, cattle, poultry, swine, and minerals. It also supports an abundant growth of fine hardwoods, notably mahogany, and softwoods such as pine. Recently, feeder roads have been built in this region to connect with the modern Inter-Ocean Highway, which links the region with both coasts. Tegucigalpa—which has a population of about 534,000 and is Honduras's largest city—is located in the highlands.

On one of the large banana plantations of the fertile inland plain, recently harvested bananas are hauled by cable from the fields to a boxing station where they will be packaged and shipped north for export.

The Banana Country

The northern end point of the Inter-Ocean Highway is at the port of Puerto Cortés, on the shore of the Caribbean. En route, a bit south of this busy port, is San Pedro Sula, which has a population of about 400,000 and is the nation's second largest city. This city, where most of Honduras's light industry is located, is one of the most rapidly growing cities in Latin America. Not far away is the small town of El Progreso, the heart of the thriving banana country.

For the most part, Honduras's huge banana plantations are situated in a flat, rich farming belt that stretches inland for about 50 miles from the shores of the Ca-

ribbean. Although this fertile region embraces only about 15 percent of the nation's land area, it supports approximately 25 percent of Honduras's total population. In its remarkably productive soil—mostly clay and sandy loam—all of the bananas exported by Honduras are grown. Significant amounts of rice, corn, beans, fruits, cattle, and poultry are also produced in this area, not for export but for consumption within Honduras.

This rich northern coastal area also boasts four of the nation's five important seaports, of which Puerto Cortés is the leading one. The only railways in the country are here as well—approximately 75 miles of rail linking the banana-growing areas with the principal ports.

The Lowlands

At the eastern end of the Caribbean coast is a region of gently rolling grasslands and forested lowlands embracing numerous swamps and lagoons. The climate is hot and muggy all year, and, although it contains about 20 percent of the nation's area, fewer than 5 percent of the nation's people live there. There are no modern highways, and transportation depends solely on mules, shallow-draft boats, and rugged four-wheel-drive trucks capable of braving the difficult jungle paths. The people of this area are occupied mostly in logging, primitive farming, and fishing the many lagoons and the coastal waters. Another lowland area lies along the Pacific coast at the Gulf of Fonseca. This coastal strip comprises only about 2 percent of the nation's land, but practically all of the nation's sesame seed and cotton are grown there.

Islands

The Bay Islands, of which the largest is Roatán, lie in the Caribbean about 30 miles off the northern coast. The islands are famous for their splendid beaches, good fishing, and crystal-clear water—as well as for the coral reefs that make them an ideal spot for skin diving and snorkeling.

Nearly 100 miles off the northern coast are the tiny Swan Islands. They were ceded to Honduras in 1971 by the United States, which had occupied them for more than 100 years despite Honduras's claim to them.

In areas where services are scarce, small streams have been tapped to supply water to local communities, in this case by cutting a long ditch through a fertile field. (Independent Picture Service)

Climate

Honduras is not subject to any noticeable seasonal change of weather. There is no spring and no autumn. Hondurans refer to only two seasons: the dry season and the wet season. The dry season starts in November and extends into April. The rest of the year is wet, with the heaviest precipitation usually taking place during September and October.

In general, the coolest time of the year is December and the warmest is May. Honduras, however, offers a considerable variety of temperature readings, depending on the location and altitude. The most pleasant year-round climate is found in the interior highlands, where the average daily temperature is between 65° and 75° F. This means that people in the highlands can sleep under a light blanket at night and wear short sleeves during the day.

To move from the interior highlands to the low-lying coastal areas is to enter a different world. From the Caribbean lowlands comes the northeast trade wind, dumping incredible quantities of rain on the coastal plains and along the northern slopes of the

Courtesy of CARE

The red-tiled roofs and white exteriors of Honduran houses in the village of Santa Cruz de Guayape provide protection from the rain and heat.

15

Until its deepwater port was completed, lighters (barges used to load and unload the cargo of heavier ships) arrived at San Lorenzo on the Gulf of Fonseca. They transported goods to boats berthed at the island port of Amapala.

coastal mountains. In these regions the annual rainfall totals more than 80 inches, and the dry season is at most only half-hearted, for these lowlands are hot and humid throughout the year. These are the real tropics, where the jungles and rain-forests extend unbroken except for the few clearings people have made.

Waterways

The ambling Ulúa River, which originates in the Comayagua Plain in western Honduras, carries a greater volume of water than any other river in the country. Flowing northward, it provides drainage for the rich banana plantations and eventually empties into the Caribbean. Shallow-draft boats may navigate the stream inland for many miles, but it is not suited for regular commercial shipping. Five smaller streams join the Ulúa to provide adequate drainage for the northern coastal area. The longest rivers are the Guayape–Patuca and the

The scarcity of roads has seriously hampered the exploitation of Honduras's natural resources.

16

Coco. The latter, which rises near the Gulf of Fonseca and flows eastward for 300 miles, is navigable by small vessels for 200 miles. Another major body of water is scenic Lake Yojoa in the interior northwest. It has no apparent outlet and is believed to have been formed by volcanic action.

Natural Resources

Because of the ruggedness of the terrain and the scarcity of roads, Honduras's mineral resources, which are not known to be large, remain virtually unexploited. Among the minerals that have been found are lead, zinc, iron, gold, copper, and silver. Commercial mines near Tegucigalpa and in Santa Bárbara have yielded enough silver, gold, lead, and zinc to export. Some people still pan for precious metals in backwoods streams, but their efforts account for less than 1 percent of the national income. Minerals from all other sources, however, amount to 6 percent of the country's exports. Timber has long been Honduras's main income-producing natural resource and is the third largest

A field crew counts the rings of a tree in Lepaterique where efforts are being made to further develop Honduras's timber export industry. The highlands have a particularly suitable climate for forestry, and new roads are being bulldozed to connect logging operations with port facilities.

17

export. Honduras is not yet a producer of petroleum, but considerable exploration for offshore oil is underway.

Flora

The vegetation of Honduras provides a pageant of brilliance throughout the year. Of particular interest are the many species of epiphytes, commonly known as "air plants"—plants that grow upon, but do not draw nourishment from, other plants. The secret of their growth is their uncanny ability to draw moisture and nourishment from the air rather than from the soil.

Courtesy of United Nations

In addition to forestry's position as an income producer, it serves to enhance the natural beauty of the countryside.

Photo by Dr. Roma Hoff

The entrance to "El Zamorano," the Pan-American Agricultural School, is appropriately lined with blooming trees in a rage of color.

Among the rich animal life found in Honduras are crocodiles who live in the swamplands and hibernate in the mud to keep cool.

They grow abundantly in the forests, where they pile up in sodden masses upon trees, crowding the leaves from tip to tip. During heavy rains, the added burden of the water that they store often becomes too much for the great tree limbs, which crash to the ground and rip out sections of the trunk as they fall.

Each of Honduras's many species of trees seems to have a favorite habitat. Pine and oak forests grow high on the rainy mountain slopes. In the eastern lowland, mangrove swamps and palm forests thrive. To the west, along the low, sandy plains, is the great pine savanna—a thin, open woodland of *Pinus caribaea.* West of the pine savanna, in the low valleys where it is rainy most of the year, is an area of dense forests. Many kinds of large trees—especially broadleaf evergreens—grow there, including mahogany, cedar, balsa, and rosewood. Castilla rubber trees can be found in these forests, as can the sapota, which yields chicle, the base of chewing gum.

It would be a tremendous task to list all the species of flowering plants in Honduras, but the most common are the orchids, the begonias, and a great variety of roses.

Fauna

Protected for centuries by impenetrable jungles and inaccessible mountain peaks, Honduran wildlife—from the common howler monkeys of the jungle to an occasional rare black panther—has remained safe from large-scale human interference. Among the mammals that thrive in Honduras are white-tailed deer, boars, tapirs, badgers, wolves, coyotes, foxes, and many members of the cat family, including jaguars, ocelots, lynxes, and pumas.

A puma—or *león*, as it is often called in Latin America—is a large carnivore of the cat family. The Honduran tapir, a horse-like animal with a small trunk, looks like a cross between an elephant and a donkey. Sometimes called "mountain cows" by the natives, tapirs flee at the slightest intrusion and are seldom seen, despite their ungainly bulk.

Wari is the Miskito Indian name for the white-lipped peccary, or *chancho de monte*, a big, low-slung relative of the hog. Roaming the rain-forest in large droves, waris give off a scent strong enough to enable hunters to track them down solely by smell. The average wari weighs from 80 to 100 pounds and yields enough meat to make it an attractive hunter's object. When frightened, however, a wari may turn and rip an attacker apart in seconds with the blunt tips of its long, curved, yellow tusks.

Smaller tree-dwelling animals abound in Honduras. The coati is a small creature

Photo by Dr. Roma Hoff

Abundant forests have long provided the wildlife of Honduras with good protection from the destructive interference of human populations and industry.

20

There are a variety of parrots in Honduras. One of the most unpredictable is the bright-plumed macaw, which is often found as a household pet, but which can be vicious with its powerful pointed beak.

White-tailed deer are found throughout the heavily wooded areas of Honduras.

similar in size and appearance to the raccoon, except that it has a longer body and a flexible snout. The kinkajou, which also has a body resembling a racoon's, has a rounded head that looks somewhat like a cat's. Kinkajous whistle as they play and fight in the treetops at night and can be easily tamed. The clowns of the forests and jungles are the screaming, screeching, extroverted monkeys. Yet a howler monkey can be very calm and quiet as it lounges and sprawls on an overhanging limb.

The quetzal, which resembles a very showy parrot but belongs to a distinct group of birds called trogons, is often called the most beautiful bird in the world. Honduran forests are home to this handsome bird, whose soft, brilliant plumage was once plucked by the Mayan Indians to adorn their ceremonial regalia. In addition to the quetzals, there are many other bright-hued species in Honduras, including the macaws of red, yellow, emerald, and blue and the green toucans with their bananalike beaks. The hummingbirds, miracles of mechanical design clothed in brilliant feathers, are scarcely larger than a man's thumb, but they are brave in defense of their rights, quarrelsome, and never still for a moment.

In the low swamplands of Honduras are many kinds of crawling reptiles: iguanas, skinks, crocodiles, caimans, and lizards. Also prevalent are many kinds of snakes, some harmless and others—like the giant boas and the fer-de-lance, sometimes called the *barba amarilla*—quite deadly. Both the caiman and the iguana lay numerous eggs in the warm sand. Many people eagerly seek these eggs, which they claim to be far tastier than ordinary poultry eggs.

The many interior streams offer numerous small fish. Spearfishing for the copper-and-black guapote, a palatable two-pound creature, is still a common way of supplying the family table with fish. The best sport fishing is to be found along the northern Caribbean, especially near the Bay Islands.

A Mayan face, formerly on a temple facade at Copán, expresses their classic ideal of beauty and is thought to be a female representation of a youthful corn goddess, perhaps in an attitude of song. The Maya often depicted corn and rain as divinities because they depended on good harvests and clement weather for sustenance.

2) History and Government

The history of Honduras can be divided into five major periods. The first period covers the time before Columbus discovered the mountainous land during his fourth and final trip to the New World in 1502. This was the time of the Maya, whose civilization even today staggers the imagination of archaeologists digging into its past. The second period is that of the Spanish conquest, during which the conquistadors, in a ruthless quest for gold and wealth, brutalized and enslaved the Indians. The third stage in Honduran history is the colonial period, nearly 300 years during which Honduras was under Spanish domination. The fourth period is that of the quest for independence, a turbulent time during which Honduras first joined a federation of other newly independent Central American states and Mexico and then had to make the difficult adjustment to total self-government. The fifth period is the twentieth century, during which Honduras has enjoyed relative stability as a nation but has contended with internal political crises and regional unrest.

Honduras Before Conquest

Many ancient temples and ruins, including recent discoveries south of Comayagua, remain to be studied before the final chapter can be written about the first inhabitants of the territory. It appears that Honduras received its first human visitors about 10,000 B.C.—first one small group of North American Indians, then other groups who drifted southward from their original home in Siberia through North and Central America.

By the time Christopher Columbus arrived in what is now Honduras on July 30, 1502, there were at least six groups populating the territory. Among these were the Lencas, of unknown origin, inhabiting much of the central portion of present-day Honduras. Nearer to the Pacific, along the Gulf of Fonseca, the Cholutecas, a tribe of Mexican origin, held sway. To the northeast and all along the coast of the Caribbean dwelt the Paya. Farther west along the coast was the territory of the Jicaques. In the swamp area along the east coast lived the Tauiras, sometimes called Miskitos (or Mosquitos), and the Sumos. The Chorti Maya lived in the northwest, where they carried on a brisk business with traders from Mexico.

A Mayan figure holding a ceremonial object with a carved cross in the middle is displayed at a museum near the ruins of Copán. The cross, an ancient Mayan symbol representing the four directions, facilitated the conversion of the Indians to the Roman Catholic faith by priests who accompanied the conquistadors.

These Chorti Maya were the descendants of one of the Western Hemisphere's most advanced—and most mysterious—societies. Near Copán and in the northwest section of Honduras, numerous ruins testify to the remarkable Mayan civilization. Originally the Maya were nomads, but after arriving in Honduras they settled down and learned to cultivate maize (corn) and other crops. In time the race developed a distinct language that is still spoken by many Mayan descendants living in Honduras today. By 500 B.C., these people were well on their way toward building a highly complex civilization, of which many aspects still remain a mystery. They were skilled builders and accomplished artists, able to to construct large villages and huge, elaborately decorated temples. During their cultural peak (after A.D. 300), they erected their most ornate temples and cities—Tikal, Uaxactún, Piedras Negras, Copán, and others.

Behind the building of these many great cities and temples of worship was the driving force of a religion that completely dominated the lives of the Mayan people. In the practice of their religion they developed an accurate and sophisticated calendar. They also became brilliant mathematicians and astronomers, inventing a number system composed of dots and bars that could be added and subtracted. The Mayan writing system was a form of hieroglyphic (picture writing) inscribed on tree bark, and among their writings was an almanac that told the most suitable days for planting crops, fishing, and hunting.

In the worship of their many gods, the Maya erected huge temples and pyramids. How the people built these enormous temples by hand defies the imagination. Some of the heavy stelae, or decorated slabs of stone, that have been found weigh as much as 65 tons, and it must have called for a lot of muscle and ingenuity to get them in-

A small grimacing figure kneels while making an offering on one of the elaborately decorated structures at Copán. The wealth of ruins in Central America and the variety of their ornamentation testify to Mayan brilliance as builders and artists.

Courtesy of Museum of Modern Art of Latin America

On a stela, or carved stone pillar, at Copán, an elderly man with a flowing beard and ornate helmet faces west toward the setting sun.

Courtesy of Museum of Modern Art of Latin America

Another Mayan monument shows their bar-and-dot system of numbers and glyphs (carved figures) used to denote periods of 20 years or eras.

to position. Over the course of hundreds of years, the Maya raised their temples higher and higher by building one temple on top of another. The domain of the Maya grew as well, ultimately embracing much of Honduras, Guatemala, and southern Mexico. Then, about A.D. 800, their civilization in Honduras crumbled, and the jungle closed in on their buildings.

The fall of the Maya and the abandonment of their large cities may have come about after a revolt by the peasants and workers against the ruling group of aristocrats. The priests and the ruling group appear to have been driven out after having lost the respect of the Mayan public, and the peasants may have attempted to rule among themselves and failed. Historians estimate that about 400,000 people resided in the larger Mayan cities. Carvings at Copán indicate that the Maya ceased building their great temples around

the year A.D. 800. The Mayan civilization appears to have fallen to ruin centuries before the conquering Spanish arrived in early 1500s. But it was not the end of the Mayan people. Their descendants survive in great number in Honduras, even though the dwellings in which they live hardly reflect the glory of their ancestors' architectural achievements.

Spanish Conquest

After Columbus landed at what is now Honduras, 22 years elapsed before the country felt the first wave of Spanish conquistadors. Thereafter, the territory became an object of dispute between the Spanish of Panama and the Spanish of Mexico.

Acting under the orders of the Spanish governor of Panama, Gil González Dávila sailed from Santo Domingo in 1524 to

After archaeologists deciphered the Mayan calendar, they were able to date the ruins of the ceremonial center at Copán in western Honduras from between A.D. 400 and A.D. 800. An American diplomat, Frederick Catherwood, bought the entire site for $50 in 1839. Today, the area is a carefully preserved and protected national park and, after Tikal in Guatemala, contains the greatest collection of Mayan ruins.

Courtesy of Museum of Modern Art of Latin America

Among the remaining buildings at Copán is a stone playing field between two temples. Here opposing teams played a strenuous and often deadly game using a hard rubber ball that was thrown through a stone hoop—akin to modern-day basketball—except that in the Mayan version one of the team captains was sacrificed after the game! (Photo by Dr. Roma Hoff)

Once the Spanish conquistadors arrived, they began to imprint their civilization on the conquered territory of the Indians by imposing the Spanish method of colonial administration, converting the natives to Roman Catholicism, building churches, mining precious metals, and laying the foundations of plantation farming.

claim the new territory for Panama. Hearing of this, Hernando Cortés, the ruling conqueror of Mexico, felt that Honduras should be a part of his territory. He sent an armed force under the command of a lieutenant, Cristóbal de Olid, to Honduras to overpower the "intruders." Olid accomplished his mission but went one step further. Obsessed with Honduras's natural resources, gold and silver included, he sought to make himself the supreme ruler of the territory, independent of Cortés. Cortés immediately countered by making a forced march from Mexico through the jungles and swamps along the unexplored Gulf of Mexico. He arrived in Honduras in 1525 to find that his followers had already executed the traitor. After establishing several new colonies, he returned to Mexico the following year, leaving other, more trustworthy lieutenants in charge of the various territories.

Although Cortés had successfully established Spanish rule throughout the land, the colonies soon started fighting among themselves over mining rights and territory. During 1536 Cortés found it necessary to send another armed expedition, under the command of Pedro de Alvarado, into Honduras to restore order. While there, Alvarado founded San Pedro Sula in the rich farming country of the Ulúa Valley. Later, Alonso Cáceres, another lieutenant sent by Cortés, founded Comayagua, which eventually became the first capital of Honduras.

The conquistadors came for gold, and for gold they were ready to kill or be killed. The Indians defended their homes and their lands as best they could, but, even though they outnumbered the Spanish, they were no match for the sharp, ruthless swords of the conquerors. Many of the proud people of the forest were killed, and many more were enslaved and forced to till the soil and dig in the mines to enrich their Spanish overlords.

The last—and most formidable—resistance encountered by the Spanish in their conquest of Honduras came from an Indian chief named Lempira. With some 30,000 followers, Lempira fought the Spanish troops until he was assassinated while attending a peace conference with the Spaniards. Honduras now preserves the memory of his bravery by imprinting his picture and name on the monetary unit of the country.

Colonial Period

In 1539, Honduras—together with adjacent parts of Central America—was placed under the jurisdiction of the Spanish authorities in Guatemala. The Honduran territory was later divided into the provinces of Tegucigalpa and Comayagua, and a governor was installed in each. During the 1570s, Tegucigalpa entered the limelight when valuable deposits of silver and gold were discovered there. With this discovery came a sharp rise in Tegucigalpa's population, and it became a rival of Comayagua in importance. Colonial development suffered as the Spanish ruthlessly exploited the mines for gold and silver. As the Indian slaves died from exhaustion, the exploiters increased their labor supply by bringing in slaves from Africa.

While the Spanish gathered more and more gold, the bands of pirates who sailed the Caribbean grew busier and busier. The

Courtesy of CARE

The conquering Spanish not only developed cities, but also organized the hundreds of village settlements that still dot the countryside. Usually, these small hamlets revolved around a village square and its centrally located church.

There were few instances of strong resistance to Spanish oppression, but Chief Lempira, commemorated in the name of and decoration on Honduran currency, headed the final stand.

buccaneers specialized in plundering the merchant ships bound for Spain with the riches of Central America aboard. The remains of some of the vessels sunk by these raiders can still be seen in the clear waters of the Caribbean near the Bay Islands and off the eastern seacoast. The pirates might also pay a call on one of the small Spanish settlements along the eastern Caribbean coast and, after drinking all the whiskey, plunder the village and burn it to the ground.

Great Britain, eager to gain a foothold on the Central American mainland, established control over the Mosquito Coast from the San Juan River in Nicaragua to what is now Belize and laid claim to the Bay Islands just off the northern coast of Honduras. It was only through intervention by the United States that Honduras was later able to reclaim the islands.

Independence

Honduran independence was achieved without bloodshed and with remarkably little commotion. On September 15, 1821, Mexico and all the Central American nations simply declared their independence from Spain, which, in a weakened condi-

tion, could do no more than accept the ultimatum in silence. Unprepared to shoulder the responsibility of self-government, Honduras was in chaos for the next 70 years. The nation suffered from internal strife and sometimes warred openly with its neighbors in boundary disputes.

Shortly after gaining freedom, Honduras, together with all the Central American nations except El Salvador, consented to being taken over by Mexico under the regime of Agustín de Iturbide. (El Salvador, in resisting the annexation, hoped to become a part of the United States, but Iturbide's troops forced El Salvador's annexation before that could happen.) Two years later the Iturbide regime collapsed, and the Central American nations broke away to form the Federation of Central America.

Manuel José Arce was nominated in 1823 to serve as the federation's first president. His hopes of cementing the five nations together under one central government proved hopeless almost from the start. General unrest caused him to resign in 1829. Francisco Morazán, a native of Honduras, was elected president of the federation in 1830. Morazán, a Liberal, headed the federation for nine stormy years. At

The second president of the ill-fated Federation of Central America was a native Honduran, Francisco Morazán, who gamely straddled the widening chasm between the Conservative pro-Church elements and the Liberal reform-minded participants in Central American politics between 1830 and 1839. His term ended with the collapse of the federation in 1839 and the eventual independence of Honduras.

this time there was a ceaseless conflict between the Roman Catholic Church, which had long dominated the political conservatives, and the liberal elements—consisting largely of Creoles (people of Spanish descent born in the Western Hemisphere)—who advocated political reforms. Although Morazán's term in office ended with the breakup of the Federation of Central America in 1839, he is a hero today throughout much of Central America. In Honduras many statues have been erected in memory of him.

After the collapse of the Central American federation, Honduras inaugurated its first constitutional president, Francisco Ferrera, on January 1, 1841, at Comayagua. Under Ferrera, a Conservative, the internal strife between the Conservatives and the Liberals intensified, and the nation's economic growth suffered as a result. Outside agitation and interference by Guatemala did not help. From 1871 to 1874, Honduras was waging war on two fronts—against El Salvador and Guatemala. The war finally ended when a bloody internal revolution broke out in Honduras. Guatemala gained a victory when its hand-picked candidate was elected president of Honduras.

In those unsettled times, Honduras seemed to be taking two steps backward for each step forward. Some definite progress, however, was made. During this period, Honduras established its first institute of higher learning—the National Autonomous University of Honduras—and in 1870 the first railroad in the country was built from Puerto Cortés to San Pedro Sula.

Marco Aurelio Soto and Luis Bográn were the two most outstanding presidents to serve Honduras in the nineteenth century. Soto worked hard to give the country a progressive administration and in 1880 managed to end the long rivalry between the cities of Tegucigalpa and Comayagua by moving the capital to Tegucigalpa. Bográn did much to put the nation's economy on a more solid footing and revived idle silver mines in the vicinity of Tegucigalpa.

Established in 1539, Tegucigalpa ("Silver Hill" in Indian) was once the site of a mining camp. In 1880, the city triumphed over its rival Comayagua to become the official Honduran capital.

The work of the executive branch of the Honduran government, despite much unrest in the twentieth century, has been conducted from the Presidential Palace, built in 1919 of heavy stone with notched battlements and turrets.

The Twentieth Century

Still smoldering with internal strife, Honduras entered the twentieth century as the poorest and least developed of all the Central American nations. The first half of the century was marked by numerous revolts and coups d'état. Political power shifted among various factions of the landowners and the military, with the U.S. government and the United Fruit Company getting involved to promote the leaders they favored. United States Marines were even sent to quell civil unrest in Honduras in 1903 and 1923. In 1937 boundary disputes with Guatemala nearly escalated to open warfare. Honduras was invaded from Guatemala in April 1945 by a group of Honduran exiles seeking to overthrow the government, but the attempt failed.

In the 1950s Honduran military officers helped the United States funnel arms to rebels who eventually toppled a left-leaning government in neighboring Guatemala. Union trouble broke out in May 1954 at United Fruit Company plantations on Honduras's north coast, only one symptom of a growing awareness in Honduras of social and economic inequality.

At this time the disagreement within the traditional oligarchy—landowners, military leaders, and foreign companies—began to give way to a reorganization of political forces. While political infighting continued to divide members of the country's conservative aristocracy, more liberal people from other segments of society looked for leaders who might enliven national politics and find effective solutions to the problems caused by Honduras's underdevelopment.

RAMON VILLEDA MORALES

One such leader was Ramón Villeda Morales, a Tegucigalpa physician who won a majority of votes in the 1954 elections. Villeda, in a three-way race, fell just short of the absolute majority required by Honduran law. Thus, he was denied the presidency until four years later, when the

legislature selected him to serve a six-year term beginning January 1, 1958.

Villeda vigorously confronted the gargantuan task of modernizing the country. When he assumed the presidency, nearly two-thirds of all Honduran adults were illiterate. Fewer than half of the children enrolled in the first grade made it to the second, and fewer than one in three wore shoes. There were few paved roads, and half of the unpaved roads were impassable during the rainy season. There was rail service for bananas, but little or none for people. The electric power grid was worse than in any Western Hemisphere nation except Haiti. The telephone system was overburdened and not to be counted on in emergencies.

With funds provided by the World Bank, Honduras began to build the Inter-Ocean Highway—the first paved highway to go from the capital to the Caribbean coast—which became the nation's main

Photo by Dr. Roma Hoff

In the mid-twentieth century many parts of Honduras were still inaccessible either because there were no roads or because the roads became impassable in poor weather. This contributed to the poverty, illiteracy, and economic underdevelopment faced by Ramón Villeda Morales when he came to power in 1954.

commercial land artery. At Villeda's prodding, a new labor code was passed, adding provisions for paid holidays and severance pay. A system of workers' insurance was put in place, drawing on contributions from employers and administered by a new Honduran Social Security Institute.

A new National Agrarian Institute was set up to redistribute the land and help settle farmers on new lands. In rural areas, Honduran farmers, encouraged by the new agencies and legislation, began to organize rural cooperatives. These groups have since grown into prosperous organi-

Much-needed agrarian reform in the 1950s and 1960s aimed to update farming methods, redistribute land to peasant ownership, and bring new fertile areas under cultivation.

Villeda's government also found the funds to build the Inter-Ocean Highway, which runs from San Lorenzo to Puerto Cortés with linkages to Tegucigalpa and San Pedro Sula—the two largest Honduran cities. Today, the nation is criss-crossed with all-weather roads that have greatly facilitated Honduran advances in education, commerce, and agrarian reform.

Courtesy of Inter-American Development Bank

zations, particularly on fertile farmlands in the northern part of the country. In 1962 Villeda pushed through the Congress of Deputies an agrarian reform law. Land acquired by the Honduran government was distributed on easy terms to landless peasants in parcels larger than five acres.

The reforms instituted by Villeda made him unpopular with traditional interests. Conservative groups of landowners attacked him on grounds that he was bringing politics into Honduran agriculture. To prevent Villeda from being succeeded by someone of his own party who held the same reformist views, the military (with strong backing from wealthy Hondurans) organized a coup d'état, and Colonel Oswaldo López Arellano proclaimed himself president.

MILITARY RULE (1963–1981)

For the next 18 years, military officers ruled Honduras. Under López Arellano, the country became embroiled with its neighbor El Salvador in a short but bloody war that left more than 1,000 people dead.

The root cause of the struggle was the illegal immigration into Honduran territory of some 300,000 land-hungry Salvadorans, who then settled mountainous areas inside the Honduran border.

In 1969 violence erupted in the capitals of both countries when national soccer teams from Honduras and El Salvador

Though El Salvador and Honduras clashed in the "Soccer War," they have not always been at odds. This plaque was sent to Honduras by the people of El Salvador to commemorate the first 100-year anniversary of Francisco Morazán's death. Morazán was head of the Federation of Central America to which both El Salvador and Honduras belonged.

A lower export tax on bananas—secured through a bribe paid to President López Arellano by the U.S. fruit company, United Brands—caused the downfall of the chief executive in 1975.

played an elimination round in the World Cup match. The third and deciding game was played in Mexico. El Salvador's team won, and frustrated Hondurans attacked Salvadoran residents in Tegucigalpa and other cities. El Salvador severed diplomatic relations and invaded Honduras. In the "Soccer War" that resulted, Honduras was accused of making aerial attacks on El Salvador. A state of war between the two nations existed until 1980, when a peace treaty was signed in Lima, Peru. The war had the unfortunate result of disrupting the Central American Common Market, a regional scheme that had dramatically increased trade and commerce in the area.

The fortresslike Presidential Palace of pale-green stone overlooks the Choluteca River in Tegucigalpa and serves as administrative headquarters of the executive branch.

López Arellano's downfall came after the damage caused by Hurricane Fifi in 1974 led to a political crisis. More than 70 percent of the banana plantations owned by one U.S. company, United Brands, were destroyed. López Arellano was accused of accepting a bribe of $1.25 million from the company in return for reducing surcharges on banana exports. He refused to be investigated and was ousted in April 1975.

In the 1980s Honduras became embroiled in international disagreements over the character and course of the Sandinista revolution in neighboring Nicaragua. Military forces of the United States used Honduras as a base of operations in the mid-1980s, as did U.S.-backed, anti-Sandinista forces called contras. Honduras also has served as a shelter for refugees. As of early 1986, more than 200,000 Nicaraguan refugees—including about 4,000 Miskito Indians—and 20,000 refugees from El Salvador had fled to Honduras from conflicts in their homelands.

Military officers continued to govern the country until 1981, when international pressure led to relatively fair elections. Roberto Suazo Córdova's assumption of the presidency in 1982 marked the return to Honduras of parliamentary democracy.

The administrative hub of San Pedro Sula is its municipal headquarters where local government affairs are decided by an elected council.

Independent Picture Service

In late 1985, an election dispute arose after Rafael Leonardo Callejas was denied the presidency—even though he had received 200,000 more votes than his opponent, José Azcona Hoyo. A Honduran election commission awarded the presidency to Azcona Hoyo because his party had received the most votes overall in balloting for national and municipal offices. Azcona Hoyo set about forming a new government, but Callejas's National party vowed to appeal the results to the Supreme Court of Honduras. The basis of their appeal is that the Honduran constitution requires a president to win a plurality of the votes cast. In any case, Azcona Hoyo became the first elected civilian in more than 50 years to succeed another elected civilian as Honduras's president

Governmental Structure

The present Honduran constitution, adopted in 1982, divides the powers of the government among the legislative, executive, and judicial branches. The executive branch is headed by the president, who is elected by direct vote of the people for a four-year term. The president appoints a cabinet of 12 ministers. There is no vice president; in case of the president's illness or death, the legislature appoints a successor. The legislature, or Congress of Deputies, is unicameral (that is, it consists of only one house). Representatives to this legislature, who are known as deputies, are elected every four years and meet annually from January 24 to October 31. The number of deputies is allocated among the country's 18 administrative areas—called departments—according to population, with each department being guaranteed at least one representative. The two major political parties are the Liberal party and the National party.

Voting is obligatory for all citizens over the age of 18, unless active military service prohibits them from participating in the electoral process. Woman gained equal political rights and voted for the first time in national elections in 1956. Men and women, however, continue to vote in separate polling stations.

The judicial powers are vested in the seven-member Supreme Court, each member of which is elected by the Congress of Deputies to serve a six-year term. The Supreme Court in turn appoints officials of the lower courts, such as appellate court judges, members of labor tribunals, and district attorneys (who name justices of the peace).

For political and administrative purposes, the nation is divided into 18 departments and a central district containing the capital. Departmental governors are appointed by the president. The municipalities within these districts elect their own local councils, since municipalities are self-governing under the constitution.

Military

The army, which has always exercised great political influence in Honduras, is under the control of the president, who holds the title of general commander. The military is legally recognized as a permanent national institution. The 1982 constitution, however—unlike its predecessors—makes no provision granting the armed forces the right to disobey presidential orders. The lack of such a provision suggests that civilian authorities have gained some power to check the actions of the military. The armed forces are responsible for defending the nation's territory and for maintaining peace and order. They also cooperate with the executive branch in activities to promote the country's development—such as in the areas of education, agrarian reform, health care, preservation of natural resources, and the extension of transportation and communication services.

Traditionally, recruitment into the armed forces consisted of military sweeps through major cities to round up men of combat age. In the early 1980s, however, military officials increased their efforts to register the 300,000 eligible men between the ages of 18 and 30. Sons of landless farmers were beginning to take a more favorable view of military service, seeing it

An aerial view shows the territory of Honduras, which the military is sworn to defend.

as an opportunity to receive new clothes, better food, and medical treatment—even as a chance to learn how to read.

Guatemala Accord

In February 1987 Costa Rican president Oscar Arias Sánchez put forth a Central American peace proposal. Arias's plan—since referred to as the Guatemala Accord—called for scheduled cease-fires, free elections, committees to solve local disagreements, and other democratic reforms. On August 7, 1987, the chief executives of Honduras, El Salvador, Nicaragua, Guatemala, and Costa Rica met to sign the accord.

Supporters of the plan are hopeful that its 90-day adjustment period will produce lasting peace in the region. Critics point to the timing of the plan, calling it a means to force foreign countries—including the United States and Cuba—to cut off their aid to Central American rebels. Other critics argue that the governments involved have no intention of meeting rebel leaders at the polling booths.

Marco Aurelio Soto, president of the Republic of Honduras from 1876 to 1883, unveiled one of the many plaques honoring Francisco Morazán to be found throughout Central America.

Nevertheless, if carried through as written, the accord would end civil wars in Nicaragua, El Salvador, and Guatemala. Furthermore, the plan would evict rebels, who are fighting guerrilla wars against those three governments, from Honduran and Costa Rican soil. Such a return of each rebel group to its own country would considerably ease international tensions in the region.

The modern National Congress building, where the Honduran legislature meets in Tegucigalpa, is built on stilts and conducts its business while the clamor of cars and buses rages beneath it.

Photo by Dr. Roma Hoff

A seller of dried flowers, helped by her children, represents one of many Honduran cottage industries. Honduras has thousands of craftspersons who work in their homes and take their products to the capital or other large towns and cities to sell.

3) The People

Honduras has a population of 4.7 million people, more than any Central American country except Guatemala. This number, however, is fewer than live in the metropolitan areas of the cities of Los Angeles and London.

In the features of modern Hondurans there are traces of the various peoples who have mingled there over the centuries—the pale skin color of the Spanish, the high cheekbones of the Maya and other Indians, and occasionally the African's dark complexion. Whereas less than a hundred years ago the Honduran Indian outnumbered all other races, those of pure Indian blood now account for only a minor percentage of the population. Intermarriage has gradually blended the races to produce a population that is now 91 percent mestizo, 4 percent pure Indian, 5 percent black, and 1 percent white.

Standard of Living

In spite of great natural wealth, Honduras is a poorly developed country. The nearest rural town may turn out to be no more than a dozen dwellings clustered near a

41

forlorn church or one-room school. The homes in these areas are made from clay or rough-hewn, unpainted boards and have palmleaf roofs and bare earthen floors. There is rarely electricity or refrigeration, and food comes directly from the fields, where people toil from early morning until night with simple implements drawn by oxen or mules. Water must be carried by mule from the nearest streams, often miles away.

The poor mountain people who live where there are few roads often make long journeys on foot. If the head of the household decides to change locations, a whole family, including children, may walk for miles through rain and mud. If a rural family's livelihood depends on selling their produce in one of the village markets, their workday may begin as early as three in the morning. The trip to the nearest marketplace may be a 20-mile walk over pathless mountain ranges. The goods for sale—perhaps chickens, straw hats, and fresh vegetables—are customarily hung from braided grass rings and carried either on a yoke or in bunches slung over a mule's back.

The diet of the rural people consists of homegrown beans, rice, and maize, together with *cuajada* (cottage cheese). Honduran women are experts at grinding maize between stones and baking the batter into delicious tortilla cakes. Other typical foods are pork, eggs, fried bananas, chili peppers, pineapples, mangoes,

The high cheekbones and the darker skin tones of Honduras's small pure-Indian population are evident in the faces of two Paya Indians. They live in Carbon, a remote village of Olancho department not far from the Nicaraguan border.

The standard of living in rural areas of Honduras is still quite low. There are few amenities available and large families typically live in small thatched dwellings along rough dirt roads.

After grinding maize (corn) into powder, Honduran women make a rough batter for tortilla cakes and cook them on wood-burning stoves.

Frying bananas is a typical way to prepare the abundant fruit, and vendors offering this delicacy are found in many large towns and cities.

Photo by Dr. Roma Hoff

papayas, berries, other tropical fruits, and nuts. Alcoholic drinks include aguardiente (a white rum), beer, and wine—including *vino de coyol,* a sparkling wine obtained from the sap of the coyol palm.

In the backwoods and mountains, old age and poverty are seldom seen together, for hardships and disease have a way of taking their toll early in life. Improvements in the standard of living for rural Hondurans have been slow in coming. Although the central government has fought the problems of poverty and illiteracy for years, not much progress has been made.

Compared to the mountain people, urban dwellers live a life of comfort. In the larger cities, where skilled work is in demand, the average head of a family is able to maintain a small home with an open patio. The daughter of such a family may work as a stenographer or bookkeeper in one of the downtown office buildings. The son of the house may be employed as a mechanic at a garage, as an employee—or even the proprietor—of one of the local filling stations, or as a salesman for one of the local chemical companies.

Yet average city dwellers enjoy only a

fraction of the conveniences familiar to their counterparts in Britain and the United States. Few Hondurans can afford a car. In the cities, traveling by taxi or city bus is much cheaper than maintaining an automobile that burns expensive imported gasoline. Air conditioners are much-appreciated appliances in the tropics—but few working people can afford the luxury of one.

Health and Social Welfare

Health conditions in Honduras vary between rural and urban areas. About 60 percent of the population lives in the countryside, where there is less access to trained medical personnel. In addition, poverty imposes restrictions on food so that the diet of rural Hondurans is often nutritionally deficient. Health problems also arise from lack of pure drinking water and poor sewage facilities.

In the cities, on the other hand, physicians and health services are readily available. In 1987, 69 out of every 1,000 Honduran babies died each year. This figure is slightly higher than the Latin American average but is the second highest in Central America.

Until recent decades there was no middle class in Honduras. A few landowners controlled most of the wealth of the nation. Workers did well to receive a few coins a day and were forced to live in miserable one-room houses. Such conditions still remain to a certain extent, but there has been some improvement since 1955. That

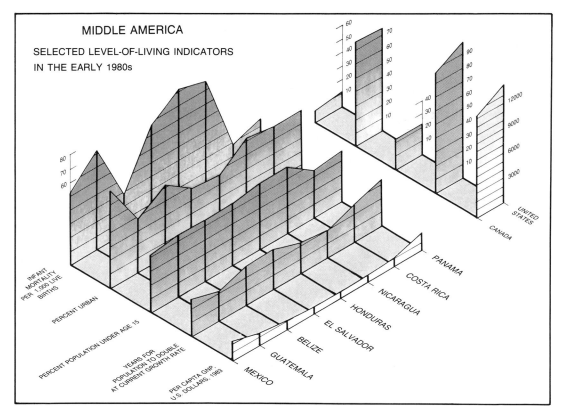

This graph shows how each of five factors, which are suggestive of the quality and style of life, varies among the eight Middle American countries. Canada and the United States are included for comparison. Data from "1986 World Population Data Sheet" (Washington, D.C.: Population Reference Bureau, Inc., 1986).

Among the noticeable improvements in the standard of living for rural Hondurans has been the availability of running water. Elsa Marina de Flores and the 300 inhabitants of her village of La Guama have been among those to benefit from a national program to make safe water available to all Hondurans.

was the year in which Honduras enacted a code that guaranteed the right to work, established minimum wages, instituted an eight-hour workday, and ensured the freedom to unionize and the right to strike for better working conditions. To this has been added a social security program. Since then the cost of living has continued to climb, especially in the urban areas, but the per capita national income has also risen. Slowly Honduras is developing a middle class, which could eventually change the character of the nation.

Education

Illiteracy has long been a major problem in all Central American nations. In Honduras the central government has attempted to combat this handicap by making schooling free and compulsory for all children from ages 7 to 15, but it is dif-

Primary school teachers take advantage of a summer course on general biology offered at the University of Honduras in Tegucigalpa. Through microscopes, the student-teachers examine chloroplasts, which produce sugar from water and carbon dioxide.

ficult to enforce attendance in the remote areas. Illiteracy rates vary greatly according to location, being very high in the rural settlements (especially in the western sections inhabited by Indians) but quite low in the highlands near the capital and in the cities along the northern coast. Although the nation's overall illiteracy rate has decreased immensely during the past decade, it still stands at about 45 percent.

In the early 1980s, 6,500 primary schools were serving more than 700,000 children. Enrollment in the 354 secondary, normal, and technical schools was about 130,000 pupils. Honduras's three universities had a total of almost 30,000

School is free and compulsory until 15 years of age in Honduras, yet more than half of the population still cannot read or write.

47

Courtesy of Inter-American Development Bank

Vocational education attracts many young Hondurans, like this student at the Luís Bográn Technical Institute of Tegucigalpa, who contours a piece of wood by operating a lathe as part of a furniture-making course.

students, and a teaching-training college had about 6,000 students. There are also several vocational schools, both private and public, some of which have adult evening classes.

Language

Although there are a few areas where the ancient tongues of the Indians still prevail, the language of Honduras is Spanish. The Spanish spoken, however, is not the aristocratic Castilian dialect taught in many North American classrooms. Honduran Spanish not only drops certain syllables but also contains many words borrowed from the Mayan language.

English-speaking groups live on the Bay Islands and are descended from the British who occupied the area in the seventeenth century. Also on these islands are descendants of the Carib Indians who came from the West Indies. These peoples speak an Indian tongue that does not sound like the Mayan language, which is used—if only by a few groups—on the Honduran mainland.

Photo by Dr. Roma Hoff

The Pan-American Agricultural School welcomes about 250 male students from Mexico and Central and South America. They follow a four-year curriculum that covers all aspects of theoretical and practical farming, from growing fruits and vegetables to courses in animal husbandry.

Eighteen-year-old Miguel Angel Uclés learns how to operate a radial saw as part of a carpentry class at the Luis Bográn Technical Institute in Tegucigalpa. The institute is one of three vocational schools built and financed by loans from the Inter-American Development Bank, which is the regional agency founded in 1959 to promote economic and social growth in Latin American countries.

Low-income families are substantially raising their standards of living by being trained at local community centers and in technical schools in useful skills such as sewing *(above)* and furniture making and repair *(right)*. (Independent Picture Service)

In Tegucigalpa's main plaza, the cathedral acts as a center of religious activity, as well as being an architectural reminder of Honduras's Spanish colonial past.

In a detail from *Palm Sunday*, Honduran primitive painter Antonio Velázquez portrays the steadfast devotion of Hondurans to the Roman Catholic faith.

Religion

Although the constitution guarantees religious freedom to everyone, approximately 98 percent of the people profess the Roman Catholic faith. In the northern coastal area near the Bay Islands there are scattered Protestant churches, with the Methodist denomination having the largest following.

Architecture

The ancient Mayan culture still influences Honduras today. Tegucigalpa's Concordia Park is dedicated to the memory of the Maya, and in the larger cities intricate carvings and designs of the pre-Columbian era have been artfully integrated with Spanish colonial architecture. These older buildings stand in sharp contrast to sleek

Courtesy of Inter-American Development Bank

Showcasing the latest building materials and technology, modern structures house an increasing number of governmental and business offices in Tegucigalpa, but retain the quaintness of shaded canteens on the pavement in front.

At Concordia Park in Tegucigalpa, a Mayan temple showing their distinctive and elaborate ornamentation has been reconstructed in miniature.

modern skyscrapers. Some examples of baroque, Renaissance, and Moorish architecture can also be found, but these are in the minority.

Music and Recreation

Honduran folklore, folk tunes, and native dances are similar to those of other Central American countries. As for modern music, many Hondurans enjoy popular dance recordings from the United States and songs in Spanish from other Latin countries. Their preferred musical instrument is the marimba, and it is not uncommon to hear the rhythms of a marimba band in full swing at any hour of the day or night. In the movie theaters of the larger cities, movies from Mexico and Hollywood are shown. Westerns are perhaps the best liked of these foreign films.

Association football (soccer) is the national sport of Honduras. To be a hero in Honduras one need only become an outstanding soccer player. Basketball continues to grow in popularity, however, and golf courses can be found in and near the larger cities.

Clothing

Smart modern attire is now considered a must for the well-dressed Honduran. Conservative townspeople and Indian women, however, still retain a fondness for the

52

Traditional costumes are worn by student folk dancers at a rural school in San Francisco, central Honduras. (Independent Picture Service)

bright traditional style of dress, which is of Mayan origin. Among Honduran young people, modern styles that are favored by teenagers throughout the rest of the world have gained some popularity.

The Arts

Of the several prominent writers and artists of Honduras, Arturo López Rodezno is perhaps the best known. To train new artists for the nation, he founded the

A student at the Tegucigalpa campus of the University of Honduras practices painting strokes during one of the classes offered in various art forms, including native handicrafts.

Courtesy of Museum of Modern Art of Latin America

Antonio Velázquez (*below left*) not only gave the world a window on rural Honduran life, he also painted urban scenes. His colorful depiction of Tegucigalpa's main square features the equestrian statue of Francisco Morazán in front of the cathedral.

Photo by Dr. Roma Hoff

National School of Arts and Crafts. Another widely known artist is the painter Antonio Velázquez (1906–1983), who is best known for paintings depicting life in and about his own little village, San Antonio de Oriente. Early Honduran writers recognized outside their own country for outstanding literature are José Cecilio del Valle, Father José Reyes, and Ramón Rosa. More recent authors include Juan Molina, Marcos Reyes, and Rafael H. Valle.

Bananas — the fruit is essential to the health of the Honduran economy.

4) The Economy

The performance of the Honduran economy is heavily influenced by the production and export of two crops, bananas and coffee. Foreign-owned companies produce most of the bananas, and local enterprises grow most of the coffee. Both groups often exert considerable pressure on national politicians to promote their interests. Up until recent years, the Honduran government has remained on the sidelines in economic matters, preferring to leave such things to the private sector.

The banana industry is a year-round activity, requiring huge investments in the physical facilities for growing bananas and in the development of a global marketing system. Honduras's banana industry was originally developed by the United Fruit Company in the beginning of the twentieth century. Today, two U.S. firms, United Brands (formerly the United Fruit Company) and the Standard Fruit Company—two of the largest corporations in Honduras—control most of the country's banana

Bananas are cultivated in large groves generally located inland from the Caribbean Sea.

Workers harvest bananas by following strip markers of colored plastic that indicate the fruit ready for the machete.

production. Together they account for more than one-quarter of the value of Honduras's total exports.

Despite its treelike appearance, the banana plant is not a tree but a gigantic herb. Like other herbs, the banana plant has no woody trunk that stands from year to year but has instead an annual main stem—that is, a stem that dies after bearing fruit. After the fruit has been harvested, the stems are cut down; new sprouts from underground, called offsets, will replace them later. Two or three of these sprouts are allowed to bear. In the humid climate, the growth of the new sprouts is so rapid that the fruit is usually ripe within 10 months of the time the new offsets begin to grow. The main stalks or stems may vary from 10 to 40 feet in height. The average cluster of bananas weighs 25 pounds, but individual bunches often exceed 40 pounds. Workers clean, sort, and grade the green bananas before carefully packing the clusters into plastic bags for export in refrigerated ships to

After harvesting, bananas are cooled in a circulating bath. They will next be sorted, boxed, labeled, and shipped—all within 12 hours.

Bananas unable to be used as whole fruit are skinned and mashed. The puree is then sold abroad to confectioneries and infant food manufacturers.

After harvesting, bananas are left on the stalk and travel in strong cellophane bags to large refrigerated ships where they are carefully loaded onto conveyor belts by teams of workers. Mature, ripe clusters can weigh more than 40 pounds.

57

Once on the conveyor, the stalks travel to cooled chambers in large export vessels. Most of Honduras's banana crop is purchased by the United States.

foreign countries. The United States, which buys more than $200 million worth of Honduran bananas annually, is Honduras's best customer.

The weather and world prices dramatically affect Honduras's earnings from bananas and coffee. Hurricane Fifi, which ravaged banana plantations along the north coast in 1974, destroyed 70 percent of the country's banana crop and caused some $200 million in damage to physical facilities. In March 1983, severe windstorms caused somewhat less damage in the same area. That same year, plant diseases deeply hurt coffee production in the departments of Choluteca and Santa Bárbara and along the western border with El Salvador. Similarly, the ups and

downs of world prices have created a boom-and-bust cycle in bananas and coffee earnings—making it difficult for Honduras to budget ahead.

Small-Scale Farming

Nearly two-thirds of the Hondurans who are a part of the money economy work in agriculture. By contrast with the large, efficient banana plantations, most Honduran small-scale farms are extremely backward. Their most important crops are corn and beans. With little training or preparation, many farmers in Honduras get meager yields from their crops, which are often planted on poorly drained land or in soil deficient in nutrients.

The country's farm population is widely dispersed. To reach them, successive Honduran governments using foreign financial aid have made substantial improvements in roads to bring these farmers into the mainstream of national commerce.

Along with the extension of roads, the government is seeking to extend the nation's public school system to rural areas. Through improvements in education, the government is hoping to alleviate the centuries-old poverty in rural areas, where most people earn but a fraction of the national per capita income of less than $600 per year.

Trade

Besides bananas and coffee, Honduras's chief exports include timber, meat, and sugar. Other less important exports are cotton, abaca (Manila hemp), tobacco, and coconuts. Leading trading partners are the United States, Trinidad and Tobago, Japan, West Germany, and Guatemala.

Courtesy of Inter-American Development Bank

At Jicaro on the south coast, salt is extracted from sea water. The sun evaporates the liquid from shallow pools leaving the crystals to be harvested with wooden rakes.

Courtesy of Inter-American Development Bank

Representatives of Finland and Honduras discuss the progress of pine-seedling growth in the Olancho department of northeastern Honduras, where the climate and soil are suitable for forestry.

Honduras imports significant amounts of fuel, lubricants, chemical products, transport equipment, and food products. In the mid-1980s the nation had a foreign debt of almost $2 billion, and the interest payments on this debt siphoned off a sizable portion of the national budget. In addition to a low per capita income figure, unemployment stood at 25 percent. Such adverse economic conditions have caused Honduras to remain one of the poorest nations in the hemisphere.

Industry

Honduran manufacturers have traditionally produced goods such as shoes, textiles, plastic items, furniture, and paint for local markets. Lately, the meat-packing and food-processing industries have grown, partly because of the high cost of imported food. It makes economic sense for Honduras to process its agricultural products at home instead of exporting raw produce only to buy it back after it has been processed elsewhere.

Workers adjust the level of a new rotary kiln that will be used in the production of cement at a plant located at Piedras Azules near Comayagua. The plant is being built with the assistance of a Japanese firm, Kawasaki Heavy Industry, Ltd., while construction is supervised by the Spanish company, Asland.

The energy producers that fuel industries in Honduras include a 292-megawatt hydroelectric project on the Humuya River. It provides electricity nationwide and controls flooding in the San Pedro Sula area. A major industrial development near Puerto Castilla involves the construction of roads, sawmills, factories, and shipping facilities to make lumber, pulp, and paper from the extensive pine forests of the Olancho department. A new deepwater port at San Lorenzo has been completed, eliminating the need for lighters—barges that ferry goods from ships to shore across shallow bays on the Gulf of Fonseca. A steel mill is planned near Agalteca, 65 miles north of Tegucigalpa, where iron and limestone are available locally.

The government is encouraging the extension of agriculture into the lower Aguán Valley, an area considered favor-

A woman employed by Milks Products of Honduras monitors a milk-bottling machine.

The quality of Honduran seedlings is being shared with other countries as agronomist Marco Flores Rodas sends pine seed samples to Africa and other parts of Latin America.

household chemicals. Honduras, with its vast supply of untouched resources and skilled workers, hopes that the growing diversity of its products will make the country's economy less vulnerable to bad weather and fluctuations in worldwide commodity prices—factors that Honduras cannot control.

able for the cultivation of basic grains and African oil palms. Eventually, factories making soap, margarine, shortening, and cooking oils from these plants may develop in this region.

Over the past 10 years, an industrial revolution has gathered strength in Honduras, particularly in the area of San Pedro Sula. Dissatisfied with their low purchasing power, the people have demanded more jobs and better wages so that they can enjoy some of the consumer goods that people in other countries take for granted. Heeding these demands, industry is gathering momentum.

Although most of the new manufacturing firms that are springing up are small, they are creating jobs and paying higher wages. As manufacturing plants increase in size and number, they should give the nation additional employment, a higher per capital income, and a better standard of living. Presently, products from small companies include beer and mineral waters, fruit juices, flour, vegetable lard, coconut oil, sweets, cigarettes, textiles and clothing, panama hats, nails, matches, plywood, cement, paper bags, soap, candles, and

Fat is extracted from milk at the San Pedro Sula dairy plant—the first in Honduras to produce dry milk. Efforts to vary the industrial base of the country have been aimed mainly at food production.

Due to treacherous terrain, some roads appear to have been cut through the mountains. This segment of road belongs to the Inter-Ocean Highway and links Tegucigalpa with the industrial city of San Pedro Sula, before it continues to the Caribbean coast.

Transportation and Communication

Although its road system is improving, Honduras has less than 2,000 miles of highway and many of the nation's roads cannot accommodate motor traffic. Blasting tunnels and building modern highways through the mountainous country is slow and expensive, but the government is using foreign aid to establish essential roadways. The United States is providing loans, grants, and technical assistance; also, a substantial World Bank loan is being used for highway improvements. The modern Inter-Ocean Highway has re- placed the narrow, hazardous road that once connected Tegucigalpa with San Pedro Sula. This very important artery also connects the capital with Puerto Cortés and other vitally important shipping points. Secondary feeder roads have been built to connect outlying areas to this highway.

Railways are confined to the north coastal region and are used mainly for transportation of bananas. Tegucigalpa, the capital, is not served by railway, and Honduras has no international railway connections.

Over a large part of the country, airplanes are the normal means of transportation for both people and products. There are international airports at Tegucigalpa, San Pedro Sula, and La Ceiba, and there are more than 30 smaller airstrips in various parts of the country.

Frequent sailings link Puerto Cortés by sea to Europe and North America. Several different lines serve the port, including vessels operated by United Brands and the Standard Fruit Company.

Honduras has four commercial television channels, and there are about 30,000 television sets in the nation to receive them. Sixty cinemas offer seating to some 60,000 persons, and four newspapers are regularly published. More than 35,000 telephones are in use.

Finance

The national unit of currency is the lempira, which since 1934 has been valued at approximately two lempiras to the U.S. dollar. The Banco Central de Honduras controls the country's banking system, having the authority to fix bank rates, to determine the legal reserve required for commercial banks, and to serve as the sole bank of issue. In addition, there are several private banks such as the Banco de Honduras, affiliated with Citibank, and the Banco Atlántida, which is affiliated with Chase Manhattan and has branches in all major cities and many towns. The Central American Bank for Economic Integration, a regional institution whose operations have been disrupted by political turbulence, has its head office in Tegucigalpa.

Honduras has begun to develop tourism, an industry with significant potential owing to the country's many scenic attractions and friendly people. The beautiful islands off the northern coast are one major area undergoing development. Another is the Gulf of Fonseca, an area known for good fishing and lovely scenery.

High gasoline prices have encouraged the use of economical Volkswagen buses as vehicles for municipal public transportation.